HUMAN DEVELOPMENT

A Guide By The Numbers
For Health and Wellness

Pierre Mouchette

Life Knowledge Media USA
Enviro | Life Knowledge Publications

ISBN 9798852293763 (Paperback Book)

Independently Published
Enviro | Life Knowledge Publications

First Edition: July 2023
Life Knowledge Media USA
https://www.enviro-life-media.com/

Disclaimer

This Enviro | Life Knowledge Publication provides information about the subject matter covered. The author and publisher of this content are not acting as licensed professionals to present the covered material. Information and statements made are for educational purposes. They are not intended to replace a one-on-one relationship with a qualified licensed health care professional. Always consult your doctor or other health care professionals before making medical decisions. You hold Life Knowledge Media USA, its subsidiaries, and its members harmless in any event, claim, demand, or damage, including reasonable attorneys' fees, asserted by any third party or arising from your use of, or conduct on, publications and products.

Life Knowledge Media USA writers provide applicable content and break-down complex topics to make them easier to understand. The information given may not apply to your specific situation, and the products or services recommended might not be a good fit for your application. Medication information contained herein is subject to change and does not cover all possible uses, precautions, warnings, drug interactions, allergic reactions, or adverse effects. An absence of warnings or other information for a given drug does not indicate that the drug or drug combination is safe, effective, or appropriate for all persons or all specific uses. While Life Knowledge Media USA strives to provide accurate, up-to-date content, we cannot guarantee the accuracy and completeness of the information supplied. By using this content, you understand that all material is an expression of opinion and not professional advice.

Life Knowledge Media USA advises the reader to keep up to date on activities in their locale by consulting with the appropriate licensed professionals for decisions that could affect them.

HUMAN DEVELOPMENT
A Guide By The Numbers For Health and Wellness

Table of Contents

INTRODUCTION

Parents need to pay attention! Children today have so many opportunities to be diverted from the challenges of growing up. Doing too much for your children may be as bad as providing no direction. It can help to explain why so many young adults suffer from anxiety and depression, have an oversize sense of entitlement, or are unable to launch. Children today face more challenges than earlier generations, so parents need to be aware.

How Is Parenting Different Today?

Prior parenting philosophies had parents overreacting, underreacting, or in denial, justifying their children's behavior, providing choices versus direction, and causing their children confusion when they required boundaries and guidance. Over the past decade, parents have had to beg and negotiate with their children, trying to get them to buy into the right thing to do. That not working, they then throw money, devices, and opportunities, creating self-indulging children with a sense of entitlement. And then, the child reaches adulthood, where their behavior and attitude have become inexcusable and unaccepted.

Currently, many adolescents, college-bound young adults, and graduates are unarmed with skillsets and coping mechanisms to deal effectively with the challenges that they are presented with. Instead, they continue to demonstrate expectations that the world will treat them like their parents and are surprised by the result. We see young adults jumping from one job or opportunity to another, taking a long time to finish college, and frequently returning home due to failed attempts at launching. These young adults have not developed the independence and ability to deal with life's challenges effectively.

In some instances, these young people exhibit depression, anxiety, panic attacks, self-harm, or make poor decisions that impact their success. Their parents were not involved early on and throughout their lives, directing, modeling, and coaching them away from the sometimes-harmful alternatives they have now turned toward.

The Challenges That Parents And Children Face

Today, children face challenges and dangers that most of us never dreamed of growing up. Online predators, mass school shootings, and cyberbullying can cause confusion, anxiety, depression, performance issues, and suicidal behavior. Additionally, they spend more time staring into screens than we could have imagined, absorbing unbelievable amounts of information. Repercussions of these influences, as well as societal pressure, impact their day-to-day lives.

The absence of support and adaptation to family dysfunction, divorce, remarriage, and the lack of parental awareness of how this impacts their child often leads to depression and anxiety, difficulty in school, and relationships as adults. Social-media influence, online pornography, substance abuse, and bullying are all alternatives some kids use to cope with heightened emotionality because parents are not paying attention. This, together with the lack of healthy coping mechanisms and the absence of positive social interaction and integration with peers, affects the way children cope with conflict and challenges they are surrounded by, leading to questions about their capability, purpose, and confidence.

So, the key to effective parenting today is flexibility, matching parental responsiveness and direction to their child's level of performance. This process must be in constant motion, evaluated, and adaptable to the child's results.

CHAPTER 1   FAMILY DYNAMICS

FAMILY

Sometimes referred to as first-degree relatives, the immediate family are the ones who are a part of your everyday life. Attempting to figure out who is a part of your immediate family may seem tricky initially, but several clear rules outline who is included.

Immediate Family Members

Your immediate family includes the following members:

- Spouse
- Parents
- Grandparents
- Children (adopted, half, and stepchildren are included)
- Grandchildren
- Siblings
- In-laws (mother, father, brother, sister, daughter, and son)

There are two ways to determine immediate and other family members. They are:

Relation by blood - means they share the same lineage or parent, such as siblings, children, or grandchildren.

Relation by marriage - means they share a common bond through the marriage of one family member, such as with in-laws or stepchildren.

THE IMPORTANCE OF FAMILY

As a child grows and develops, their earliest interactions are typically with family members and associated caregivers. These initial contacts are vital for the development of the child's socialization skills as well as teaching children how to get a better understanding of themselves and those around them.

Since children learn by observing family members and caregivers, they are also the prominent influencers that determine how a child will socialize and learn, contributing to their overall physical, social, and intellectual development. Having a loving family and caregivers around helps the child build a solid foundation that will affect future relationships, work, health, and a sense of self.

Family Bonds Begin At Birth

When a child is born with a loving family and caregivers, they achieve a crucial development skill out of attachments. When a baby is held, cradled, soothed, and quickly fed or changed, these bonds of affection and nurturing help build healthy parent/caregiver-child relationships. As infants successfully attach to their caregivers and other family members (including siblings and grandparents), they learn to trust and are more likely to explore and engage with others. Such relationships help build a lifetime of trust, intellectual development, and learning rules of behavior associated with high self-esteem, better performance in school, and less adverse outcomes, such as depression or drug use, later in life.

Developmental Skills

Once a baby is born, family members and caregivers may play a significant role in the child's overall development as follows:

Building motor skills - involves such learned behavior as how to sit up, walk, run, climb, hold a cup, and more. These skills may seem basic, and not something you teach, but the parent or caregiver is accountable for teaching these skills to the child at a young age. As a child learns motor skills, they will help the child feel independent and lead to their overall development.

Building language skills - parents and caregivers should always talk to their children, even as infants. If a child cannot yet respond, they are most definitely listening and learning when they hear adults speak to them.

Building emotional skills - is very important to help a young child develop emotional skills, and parents and other adult caregivers should be the earliest teachers. By teaching a child essential skills like smiling or waving at others, they may learn to be open to others. Educating young children on basic emotions and naming their fear and love can also help them learn to describe their feelings and be better at expressing themselves. As they age, teaching emotional skills such as sympathy, compassion, and sharing can help a child have an emotionally healthy life and to be more grounded when dealing with the highs and lows of life.

Family values - as the infant ages, they begin to understand the meaning of right or wrong. Parents, family members, and other caregivers are the best teachers for these lessons, and they can help a child establish their own set of personal values and norms. Again, because the child learns from watching others, adults play a crucial role in modeling behavior. When a child sees the adults in their life treat others with respect, kindness, and responsibility, they begin to model their behaviors similarly. Parents, family, and caregivers should also discuss openly with children and ask them what they think are good values and ones that may not serve them well. From teaching responsibilities like cleaning their room or showing compassion to someone not feeling well, children will use these values as they grow into adults.

Security - because a child relies on adults to meet their basic needs like clothing, food, and shelter, they develop their primary sense of security from their parents, family members, and other caregivers. Beyond that, a child also receives their first sense of emotional security from their family members and caregivers. Setting schedules is one of the best ways to make a child feel secure. When a child knows that they will eat, sleep, bathe, or wake at a particular time, they become comfortable and confident in understanding that their needs are met.

In a secure home setting, a child will also learn how to be comfortable with who they are and to feel free to express themselves without judgment. When a parent, family members, or caregivers provide a safe, open environment, a child will feel secure and develop in a physically and emotionally healthy manner.

A parent or caregiver and other family members can be a child's most significant early teachers and influencers in setting the foundation for a healthy and happy life by establishing attachment, teaching development skills, and instilling values and a sense of security.

CHAPTER 2   HUMAN DEVELOPMENT

HUMAN DEVELOPMENT
A Guide By The Numbers For Health and Wellness

GENERATIONS

The latest definition of the generations are:

GENERATION	BORN	AGE RANGE
Silent Generation	1928-1945	78-95 years old
Baby Boomers	1946-1964	59-77 years old
Gen X	1965-1980	43-58 years old
Millennials	1981-1996	27-42 years old
Gen Z	1997-2012	11-26 years old
Gen Alpha	2010s-2025	0 to 10 years old

FYI

For New Parents

What is The Difference Between a Newborn and a Neonate?
A newborn is an infant that is just hours, days, or up to one month old. In medical contexts, a newborn or neonate (from the Latin neonatus, newborn) refers to an infant in the first 28 days after birth. The term applies to premature, full-term, and post-mature infants.

What is The Difference Between a Neonatal and a Pediatric in Hospital Healthcare?
One of the most considerable distinctions between a **Pediatric Intensive Care Unit (PICU)** and a **Neonatal Intensive Care Unit (NICU)** is that the PICU provides care for infants and children up to age 17. A NICU specializes solely in the treatment of newborns who need more TLC.

PERIODS OF HUMAN DEVELOPMENT

Prenatal Development

After conception, the three stages of prenatal development begin Germinal, Embryonic, and Fetal periods. With all of the major structures of the body forming, the mother's health is of primary concern. The influences of nature (genetics) and nurture (nutrition and teratogens, environmental factors during pregnancy that can lead to congenital disabilities) are evident.

Infancy and Toddlerhood

The first year and a half to two years of life are ones of extraordinary growth and change. Newborn babies, with numerous involuntary reflexes and a keen sense of hearing but poor vision, are transformed into walking and talking toddlers within a relatively short period. Caregivers similarly change their roles from those who manage feeding and sleep schedules to moving guides and safety inspectors for these mobile, energetic children. Brain development takes place at a remarkable rate, as does physical growth and language development. Infants have their temperaments and approaches to play. Interactions with primary caregivers undertake changes influenced by possible separation anxiety and the development of attachment patterns. Sociocultural issues center around breastfeeding or formula-feeding, sleeping in cribs or the bed with parents, toilet training, and whether to get vaccinations.

Early Childhood

Early childhood, also called the preschool years, follows toddlerhood, and precedes conventional schooling, generally from ages 2 to 5 or 6. As a preschooler, the child is engaged in learning language (with incredible vocabulary growth), gaining a sense of self and greater independence, and beginning to learn the workings of the physical world. However, this knowledge does not come quickly, and preschoolers may initially possess interesting conceptions of size, time, space, and distance. A toddler's resolve to do something could give way to the four-year-old's guilt for doing anything that brings the disapproval of others.

Middle Childhood
The ages of 6 to 11 comprise middle childhood, and much of what children experience at this age is attached to their involvement in the early grades of school. Now the world has become one of learning, testing new academic skills, and assessing their abilities and accomplishments by comparing oneself and others. Schools participate by comparing the students and making the comparisons public through team sports, test scores, and other recognition methods. The brain reaches adult size around age seven but continues to develop. Growth rates slow down, and children can refine their motor skills at this point in life. Children also learn more about social relationships beyond the family by interacting with friends and fellow students. Same-sex friendships are especially salient during this period.

Adolescence
A dramatic physical change marked by an overall physical growth spurt and sexual maturation is known as puberty. Timing can vary depending on gender, cohort, and culture. It is a time of cognitive change. The adolescent begins to imagine new possibilities and to consider abstract concepts like love, fear, and freedom. Ironically, adolescents have a conception of invincibility which puts them at greater risk of dying from an

accident or contracting sexually transmitted infections that can have lifelong consequences. A primary developmental task during adolescence involves establishing one's own identity. Teenagers typically struggle to become more independent from their parents. Peers become more critical as teens strive for belonging and acceptance; mixed-sex peer groups become common. New roles and responsibilities are being explored, including dating, driving, working part-time, and planning for future academics.

Early Adulthood

Late teens, twenties, and thirties are often considered early adulthood. It is when we are at our physiological peak but at the most considerable risk for involvement in violent crime and substance abuse. It is a time of focusing on the future and placing all energies into making choices that will earn the status of an adult in the eyes of others. Love and work are primary concerns at this stage of life. In recent years, it has been observed that young adults are taking longer to grow up in the U.S. and other developed countries. They will wait longer to move out independently, finish their education, take on a work/career, get married, and have children. Cohorts, culture, time in history, the economy, and socioeconomic status may be critical factors when youth take on adult roles.

Middle Adulthood

The late thirties (or age 40) through the mid-60s is called middle adulthood or midlife. It is a period in which physiological aging becomes more noticeable and a period at which many are at their peak of productivity. It may be a period of gaining expertise in specific fields, understanding problems, and finding solutions more effectively than before. It can also be the time to become more realistic about life possibilities and recognize the difference between what is possible and what is likely. Known as the sandwich generation, middle-aged adults could be caring for their children and aging parents. While caring about others and their future, middle-aged adults may question their mortality, goals, and commitments while not necessarily experiencing a mid-life crisis.

Late Adulthood

Life expectancy has increased in the last 100 years, especially in industrialized countries. Late adulthood crosses a wide age range with many variations, so it may be helpful to divide it into categories such as **"young-old"** (65-74 years old), **"old-old"** (75-84 years old), and **"oldest-old"** (85+ years old). The **young-old** resemble middle-aged adults, possibly still working, married, relatively healthy, and active. The **old-old** have health problems and challenges with daily living activities, and the **oldest-old** are often frail and need long-term care. However, there are many factors involved, and a better way to appreciate the diversity of older adults is to go beyond chronological age and examine whether a person is experiencing optimal aging and continues to have an active, stimulating life with **normal aging** (changes will be similar to most of those of the same age), or **impaired aging** (someone who has more physical challenges and disease than others of the same age).

Death and Dying

Yes, there is a certain discomfort in thinking about death, but confidence and acceptance can come from studying death and dying. Age, religion, and culture are important in attitudes and approaches to death and dying. There are various types of death: physiological, psychological, and social. Death's most common causes vary by age, gender, race, and culture. Death and grieving are processes and may share certain stages of reactions to loss. Cultural variations in the death rituals, mourning, and grief are abundant, with the concept of a good death described as including personal choices and the involvement of loved ones through the process.

Palliative care is an approach to maintaining the moribund (dying) individuals' comfort level. Hospice is a movement and practice involving professional and volunteer care and loved ones. Controversy surrounds euthanasia, helping people fulfill their wish to die, active and passive types, physician-assisted suicide, and legalities that vary within the United States.

AGE RANGE OF HUMAN DEVELOPMENT

Which stage of life is the most important?   Some might claim that infancy is a crucial stage when the baby's brain is wide open to new experiences that will influence the rest of its later life. Others might argue that physical health peaks in adolescence or young adulthood. Many cultures worldwide value late adulthood more than any other, arguing that at this stage, the individual has finally acquired the wisdom necessary to guide others.

Who is right? The truth is that every stage of life is equally significant and necessary.

NAME	AKA	AGE RANGE
Neonates	Newborn	Birth to 4 weeks
Infancy	Baby	0 mo. to 1yr.
	Toddler	1 - 3
Children	Early Childhood (Preschooler)	3 - 5
	Middle Childhood	6 - 8
	Late Childhood	9 - 12
Adolescence	Teenager	13 - 17
Early Adulthood	Young Adults	18 - 39
Middle Adulthood	Midlife	40 - 64
Older Adults	Mature	65 - 80
Late Adulthood	Elder or Senior	80+

STAGES OF HUMAN DEVELOPMENT

Infancy - Trust vs. Mistrust

In the first stage of human development, infants learn to trust based on how well their caregivers meet their basic needs and respond when they cry. If an infant cries out to be fed, the parent can either complete their need by feeding and comforting the infant or not meeting it by ignoring the infant. When their needs are met, infants learn that relying on others is safe; when their needs go unmet, they grow up less trusting.

Toddlerhood - Autonomy vs. Shame and Doubt

In addition to autonomy versus shame and doubt, another way to think of the second stage is independence versus dependence. Like the first stage, toddlers go through this stage responding to their caregivers. If caregivers encourage them to be independent and explore the world, toddlers will grow up with a sense of self-efficacy. If the caregivers hover excessively or encourage dependence, these toddlers become less confident in their abilities.

Preschool Years - Initiative vs. Guilt

During the preschool years, children learn to assert themselves and speak up when they need something. Some children may say they are sad because a friend stole their toy. If this assertiveness is greeted with a positive reaction, they learn that taking the initiative is helpful behavior. However, if they are made to feel guilty or ashamed of their assertiveness, they may grow up to be timid and less likely to take the lead.

Early School Years - Industry vs. Inferiority

When children begin school, they start to compare themselves with peers. If children feel accomplished in relation to peers, they develop strong self-esteem. If they notice that other children have met milestones that they have not, they may struggle with self-esteem.

Adolescence - Identity vs. Role Confusion

The term identity crisis originated in adolescence, and for a good reason. Adolescence is all about developing a sense of self. Adolescents who identify who they are, grow up with more important goals and self-knowledge than those teenagers who struggle to break free of their parents' or friends' influences. Adolescents who still depend on their parents for social interaction and guidance may experience more role confusion than teenagers who pursue their interests.

Young Adulthood - Intimacy vs. Isolation

In young adulthood, roughly at age 20, people solidify their lifelong bonds. Many enter committed relationships or marriages, while others form lifelong friendships. People who create and maintain these relationships reap the emotional benefits, while those who struggle to maintain relationships may suffer from isolation. A young adult who develops strong friendships in college may feel more intimacy than one who works to form and maintain close friendships.

Middle Adulthood - Generativity vs. Stagnation

In middle adulthood, people tend to struggle with their contributions to society. They may be busy raising children or pursuing careers. Those who feel they are contributing experience generativity, the sense of leaving a legacy. On the other hand, those who do not think that their work or lives matter may experience feelings of stagnation. For example, a middle-aged adult raising a family while working a career that presumably helps people can feel more fulfilled than an adult working a meaningless job.

Late Adulthood - Integrity vs. Despair

As adults reach the end of life, they reflect on their lives. Adults who feel fulfilled by their lives through a successful family or a meaningful career achieve ego integrity, where they can face aging and dying with peace. Older adults risk falling into despair if they do not feel they have lived a good life.

CONTRIBUTIONS BY STAGES OF LIFE

Prebirth (Potential) - the child who has not yet been born can become anything and therefore holds for all of humanity the principle of what we all may yet become in life.

Birth (Hope) - when a child is born, it instills a sense of optimism in its parents and other caregivers. A feeling that this new life will bring something unique and special into the world. Hence, the newborn represents the sense of hope we all nourish inside ourselves to make the world a better place.

Infancy (Vitality) - the infant is a vibrant and seemingly unlimited energy source. Babies thus represent the inner human dynamo, continually fueling the fires of life.

Early Childhood (Playfulness) - children recreate the world anew when they play. They take what is and combine it with what is possible to fashion events that have never been seen before. As such, they embody the innovation and transformation principle underlying every creative act.

Middle Childhood (Imagination) - the sense of an inner individual develops for the first time, and this individual is alive with images from the outer world and brought up from the depths of their subconscious. These images are the source of creative inspiration in the future for artists, writers, scientists, and anyone who finds their days and nights enriched by having nurtured a deep inner life.

Late Childhood (Ingenuity) - older children have acquired a broad spectrum of social and technical skills that enable them to invent strategies and creative solutions to the increasing pressures placed on them. This principle of ingenuity lives on in that part of us, looking for new ways to solve problems and cope with everyday responsibilities.

Adolescence (Passion) - the biological happening of puberty unleashes a robust set of transformations in the adolescent body that reflect themselves in the teenager's sexual, emotional, cultural, and spiritual passion. Adolescent passion thus represents a significant touchstone for anyone seeking to reconnect with their most profound inner zeal for life.

Young Adult (Enterprise) - it will take enterprise for the young adult to accomplish their many responsibilities. It includes finding a home and mate, establishing a family or circle of friends, and obtaining a good job. Such a principle of enterprise serves us at any stage when we must go out into the world and make our mark.

Midlife (Contemplation) - after following society's script designed for creating a life, those in midlife often take a break from worldly responsibilities to reflect on the deeper meaning of their lives and then forge ahead with a new understanding. This element of contemplation represents a vital resource we all can draw upon to deepen and enrich our lives at any age.

Mature Adulthood (Benevolence) - those in mature adulthood have raised families, settled in their work life, and hopefully, they contribute to society's betterment.

Late Adulthood (Wisdom) - having had a long life, these elders have acquired a rich repository of experiences that they can use to help guide others. Elders thus represent the source of wisdom in each of us, helping us avoid past mistakes while reaping the benefits of life's lessons.

Death and Dying (Life) - those in our lives who are dying or have died teach us the value of life. They remind us not to take our lives for granted but to live every moment of life to its fullest and to remember that our lives form a part of a greater whole.

NOTE	Each life stage has a unique gift to give to family, friends, and humanity. We should all protect the wisdom of our elders.

- 28 -

CHAPTER 3   FACTS OF LIFE

FEEDING YOUR BABY

All parents want the best for their babies. When infants begin to eat solid foods, essential nutrients, and minerals help their brains develop and flourish.

On February 4, 2021, a U.S. Congress subcommittee released a report stating that some baby foods contained toxic heavy metals such as arsenic, lead, cadmium, and mercury, a significant concern because even small amounts of these heavy metals can affect a child's growing brain.

The FDA, to date, is working to remove these metals from baby food products. In the meantime, avoiding certain baby foods can keep babies safe from heavy metals. You should know the following about heavy metals in baby foods and how to choose safe foods for your baby.

How Heavy Metals Get Into The Food Supply

Heavy metals include lead, mercury, cadmium, and arsenic. They occur naturally in the environment and are in soil and water worldwide. There has been a significant increase in heavy metal deposits over time because of air and water pollution. These metals get into the food supply because, as plants grow, they absorb these metals from the soil and water.

How much heavy metal contamination ends up in the food supply depends on several factors:

- Some plants, like rice, soak up more heavy metals as part of their growing process.

- Some areas of the world have more heavy metals in the ground than other areas. So, the food grown in these areas will have higher levels.

- Some additives, like vitamin premixes, spices, and enzymes, contain heavy metals.

What Happens If Your Baby Eats Food With Heavy Metals?
The body does not use heavy metals, and they cause toxic effects, even at low levels. Children's brains are uniquely vulnerable to damage from toxic substances because they are still developing. Also, because children are smaller than adults, the same amount of heavy-metal contamination affects a child more than adults.

Which Baby Foods Have Heavy Metals In Them?
When Congress began investigating heavy metals in baby foods in 2019, they asked seven major baby food companies to submit data to their subcommittee. These companies included:

- Beech-Nut
- Earth's Best (Hain Celestial)
- Gerber
- Happy Baby (Nurture)
- Parent's Choice (Walmart)
- Plum Organics (Campbell Soup Company)
- Sprout

Only Beech-Nut, Gerber, Earth's Best, and Happy Baby provided data. These companies gave Congress information about how they tested their foods for heavy metals, whether they tested ingredients or the finished product, and what limits they set for testing.

The data showed the following:

- Apple and other fruit juices contain arsenic
- Carrots and sweet potatoes contain cadmium and lead
- Grape and apple juice have lead
- Infant rice cereal had high arsenic, lead, cadmium, and mercury levels
- Rice-based snacks contain arsenic, lead, and cadmium

Beech-Nut later recalled some of its rice cereal in June 2021. The company also decided to stop making single-grain rice cereal products. Once the initial report became public, the remaining three companies provided data to Congress. Another report was issued on September 29, 2021, again showing these companies have high levels of heavy metals in baby foods.

Are Organic Baby Food Brands Any Safer?

Many baby foods tested for the congressional report came from companies that listed their foods or ingredients as "organic." While organic products have fewer pesticides, they can still contain these heavy metals, depending on where they are grown. Also, organic baby foods contain brown rice, which naturally has higher levels of arsenic than other types of rice.

Which Baby Foods Are Heavy-Metal Safe?

Some baby food companies are working on eliminating more heavy metals from their products. But right now, no baby food company has heavy metal-free products.

To address the problem, the FDA developed the action plan **Closer to Zero.** But, the changes will take several years to implement. Until then, experts recommend that parents limit babies' exposure to heavy metals in baby foods.

How To Limit Your Baby's Exposure To Heavy Metals
The good news is that there are easy switches you can make to decrease the amount of heavy metals your child is exposed to. Studies show that making a few simple changes can reduce the number of heavy metals babies are exposed to by 80%.

Make purees - you can create baby food by making a puree of your table foods. But making your food does not guarantee that your child will not be exposed to heavy metals. It is because heavy metals can be found in the entire food chain, not just baby foods. Limiting repeated exposure by offering various fruits and vegetables is the best solution.

Avoid white and brown rice, rice-based snacks, and rice flour. Rice absorbs more arsenic as it grows than other grains, such as oats, wheat, and bran. Limiting how much rice a baby eats will decrease exposure to arsenic.

The following are some simple switches parents can try:

- Use a cold banana or chilled cucumber instead of rice-based teethers.

- Use oatmeal, quinoa, or barley-based infant cereal instead of rice cereal.

- Choose rice with lower natural arsenic content, like basmati and sushi rice.

- Avoid rice-based snacks, like puffs. Instead, try yogurts, cheeses, or soft fruits, like applesauce, peaches, and bananas.

Limit Carrots And Sweet Potatoes

Carrots and sweet potatoes are root vegetables that absorb more heavy metals. They also provide a good source of nutrients and fiber, so do not eliminate them from your child's diet.

Offer Water Instead Of Juice

Kids like juice because it tastes good! But **Consumer Reports** found that many commercial juices also had arsenic, lead, and mercury. The **American Academy of Pediatrics (AAP)** recommends that children avoid juice for the first year of life because the high sugar content adds unnecessary calories, leading to more cavities. The heavy metals in juice are another reason to follow this recommendation.

Read Labels

Check food labels for rice or rice flour and added ingredients, like sweet potatoes. Avoid feeding your child a diet that contains too many of these items. Remember, these ingredients might not be listed as the first ingredient, so you may have to read through numerous ingredients.

Should You Have Your Baby Tested For Heavy Metals?

Testing for heavy metals is not recommended. Blood, hair, and nail tests for heavy metals are often difficult to interpret since they do not always have set reference ranges like other lab tests. Lead screening in children is the one exception to testing for heavy metals. Because lead has known toxic effects at even low levels, the AAP recommends screening for lead in children 12 to 24 months of age.

TEENS, GENES, and FOOD CHOICES

What Contributes to Adolescent Obesity?

Health care professionals may be able to help adolescents prevent obesity from becoming an unwanted side effect in their unique growth period to adulthood.

How Critical Is Adolescent Obesity?

Based on current data, almost 21 percent of adolescents ages 12–19 are affected by obesity. The obesity rate among all populations has increased steadily, although there is some evidence, at least with childhood obesity, that it is starting to level off. Yes, there is much that can be done to decrease the amount of childhood and adolescent obesity.

Obesity Risk For Type 2 Diabetes?

There is plenty of evidence that has linked obesity to Type 2 diabetes. Teens and even younger children who have obesity are at a higher risk. These children develop insulin sensitivity, and you start to see changes in their hemoglobin A1C. When you see this, it is essential to intervene with nutrition information because there might still be time to prevent Type 2 from developing. It is vital because the consequences of Type 2 diabetes and its associated comorbidities are detrimental to health.

Besides the rapid growth they are experiencing, adolescents are also undergoing changes in brain development. They are starting to make choices about whether to eat good or bad foods and are experiencing a lot of peer pressure with those decisions. They are also experiencing hormonal changes that might give them stronger cravings for certain foods.

During adolescence, you would expect increased physical activity, but in the era in which we live, many adolescents are sedentary. For example, most are playing video games instead of being active.

Environmental Factors And Adolescent Obesity

Socioeconomic status is one of the predictors of obesity. It is interesting because, in the United States, adolescents of lower socioeconomic status are much more likely to develop obesity. In contrast, it is the opposite if you look at adolescents in low-resource countries. Children with higher socioeconomic status are more affected by obesity. That could be because money may give access to fast food in those low-resource countries. But here, it is cheaper to buy fast foods than healthy foods.

Genetic Influences On Obesity

Several genes are associated with a higher risk for obesity. Genetic variables are associated with body size, body mass index, waist circumference, and appetite. Previously we were taught that the genes you were born with are the genes you are stuck with. However, now we know that the environment influences the genome, creating epigenetic changes that affect obesity. Therefore, studying the adolescent group separately from children or adults is essential. We know we are born with specific genes, but we also understand that the environment affects and interacts with our genes. So ultimately, it is the combination of our genes and environment that determines our health. For example, eating healthy foods may reduce our genetic risk for disease.

HIGH BLOOD PRESSURE IN CHILDREN

Blood pressure measures the force applied against the inner walls of the arteries as the heart pumps blood throughout the body. High blood pressure (hypertension) is an increase in this force. High blood pressure in children is usually a result of being overweight.

Blood pressures are presented as two numbers, written like this: 120/80. Either or both numbers can be too high.

- The first number is the systolic blood pressure
- The second number is the diastolic pressure

Elevated blood pressure in children up to age 13 is measured differently than in adults. It is because **blood pressure** changes as the child grows. Children's blood pressure numbers are compared with the blood pressure measurements of other children of the same age, height, and sex.

The government publishes blood pressure ranges among children ages 1 to 13 years. Abnormal blood pressure measurements are described as follows:

- Elevated blood pressure
- Stage 1 high blood pressure
- Stage 2 high blood pressure

Children older than 13 are subject to the same standard as an adult.

Causes - several issues have an impact on blood pressure, including:

- Hormone levels
- The health of the nervous system, heart, and blood vessels

- The health of the kidneys

Most of the time, a reason for high blood pressure will not be found. It is known as primary (essential) hypertension. Still, certain factors can increase the risk of high blood pressure in children:

- African Americans are at an increased risk for high blood pressure
- Being overweight or obese
- Family history of high blood pressure
- For most children, high blood pressure is connected to being overweight.
- Having high cholesterol
- Having Type 2 diabetes or high blood sugar
- History of preterm birth or low birth weight
- Issues with breathing during sleep, such as snoring or sleep apnea
- Kidney disease

A medicine may also cause high blood pressure that the child is taking. Secondary causes are common in infants and young children. These causes include:

- Certain tumors
- Heart problems
- Kidney problems
- Medicines such as steroids, NSAIDs, and some common cold medicines
- Sleep apnea
- Thyroid problems

High blood pressure will return to normal when the medication is suspended or when the condition is treated.

Symptoms - most children have no symptoms of high blood pressure. It is often discovered during a checkup when the provider checks your child's blood pressure.

Exams and tests - in most cases, the measurement is the only sign of high blood pressure. Blood pressure should be taken yearly for healthy-weight children starting at age 3. Your child's doctor will use a blood pressure cuff that fits your child correctly to obtain an accurate reading. If the child's blood pressure is elevated, the provider will measure the blood pressure twice and then use an average of the two readings.

Blood pressure should be taken at every visit for children who:

- Are obese
- Have diabetes
- Have kidney disease
- Have problems with blood vessels leading to the heart
- Take medicines that raise blood pressure

The doctor will measure your child's blood pressure many times before diagnosing high blood pressure. Additionally, the doctor will ask for more information about family history, your child's sleep history, risk factors, and diet. The doctor will give a physical exam to look for signs of heart disease, eye damage, and other changes in your child's body.

Other tests your child's provider may want include:

- Blood and urine tests
- Blood sugar test
- Echocardiogram
- Sleep study to detect sleep apnea
- Ultrasound of the kidneys

Treatment - the goal is to reduce high blood pressure so your child has a lower risk of complications. Your child's provider will tell you what your child's blood pressure objectives should be.

If your child has elevated high blood pressure, the provider will recommend lifestyle changes to help lower the blood pressure. Healthy habits will help your child not to gain more weight, lose excess weight, and lower blood pressure. Working as a family is the best way to help a child lose weight. Work with each other by:

- Following the **DASH diet,** which is low in salt, requires fruits and vegetables, lean meats, whole grains, and low-fat or non-fat dairy

- Cut back on sugary drinks and foods with added sugar

- Get 30 to 60 minutes of exercise every day

- Limit screen time and other sedentary activities to less than 2 hours daily

- Get plenty of sleep

Your child's blood pressure will be rechecked in six months, and if the pressure is still high, it will be rechecked in the child's limbs. After that, blood pressure will be rechecked at 12 months. If the blood pressure remains high, the provider may recommend monitoring continuously over 24 to 48 hours (ambulatory blood pressure monitoring). Your child may also need to see a heart or kidney doctor.

Tests can look for the following:

- Diabetes (A1C test)
- Heart disease (echocardiogram or electrocardiogram)

- High cholesterol level
- Kidney disease (a basic metabolic panel and urinalysis or ultrasound of the kidneys)

The exact process will happen for children with stage 1 or 2 high blood pressure. However, follow-up testing and specialist referral will occur at 1 to 2 weeks for stage 1 high blood pressure and then after 1 week for stage 2 high blood pressure.

If lifestyle changes do not work or your child has other risk factors, your child may need medications for high blood pressure. Drugs used most often consist of:

- Angiotensin-converting enzyme inhibitors
- Angiotensin receptor blockers
- Beta-blockers
- Calcium channel blockers
- Diuretics

Your child's provider may advise monitoring your child's blood pressure at home. Home monitoring will show if lifestyle changes or medications are working.

Outlook (prognosis) - most of the time, elevated blood pressure in children can be controlled by lifestyle changes and medicine, if necessary.

Possible complications - untreated high blood pressure in children could lead to difficulties in adulthood, which may include:

- Heart attack
- Heart failure
- Kidney disease
- Stroke

Contact Your Child's Medical Professional
Call your child's provider if home monitoring indicates the child's blood pressure remains high.

Prevention - the child's provider will evaluate your child's blood pressure at least once a year, beginning at age 3. You can help prevent high blood pressure by implementing lifestyle changes devised to bring blood pressure down. Reference to a pediatric nephrologist may be recommended for children and adolescents with hypertension.

- 42 -

CHAPTER 4   LIVING LIFE

OVERLOOKED HYGIENE MISTAKES

Parents everywhere start teaching their children personal hygiene habits when they are young. Everything from brushing their teeth, bathing, putting on clean clothes, to washing their face. It is ingrained at a very early age.

However, as time passes, we learn more about germs and how they work. What we thought was healthy years ago, we now know, in many situations, does not work. Some of the things you were taught might do more harm than good. This section will touch on what we now know for today's parents to impart to their children.

Antibacterial soaps - due to marketing, many people believe that regular soap and water does not kill germs and that we need antibacterial soaps. This is untrue. Antibacterial soaps are unnecessary and can cause more harm than good. The antibacterial compound put in soaps, **triclosan,** kills bacteria and human cells. Triclosan interrupts the body's natural production of hormones and has led to an increase in antibiotic-resistant bacteria. Plain soap and water kill germs, and triclosan is not needed. *Purchase products that do not contain this health-damaging compound.*

Antiperspirant - sounds like a good idea, and most people would not dream of leaving the house without using it, but it is one of the worst things you can use. These personal care products work through aluminum chloralhydrate, an aluminum type that is absorbed directly into the bloodstream through your skin. It then collects in the brain, increasing the chances of developing dementia and Alzheimer's. Fortunately, there are natural ways to stop odor and limit the amount of perspiration. *Try making your antiperspirant, and your brain will be glad you did.*

Flossing - yes, flossing is gross. Your gums bleed when you do not floss for an extended period. Are you aware that not flossing can lead to heart disease? It seems like a strange connection, but it is true. Bacteria stay between your teeth and deep into your gums when you do not floss. Bacteria like to travel, so they ride through the bloodstream and end up in your heart, where they can multiply, causing heart disease. They can travel to other places as well. It might be gross, but flossing once every night before bed will do much good for your teeth and heart.

Only using a vacuum - many viruses, including the Norwalk virus (stomach flu) and norovirus (which causes severe digestive distress), can live on your carpets and rugs for at least a month. Vacuuming is excellent in picking up some types of bacteria, dirt, or food particles, but vacuuming is useless against a virus. Use a steam cleaner or a disinfecting spray regularly. *If you have rugs, disinfect them regularly to kill viruses.*

Over-bathing - you most likely were taught that you need a bath every day. Some parents are known to advocate bathing twice a day. Of course, the interest is apparent. Eliminating dirt, bacteria, sweat, and stinky things from the body sounds like a great idea. But what your parents did not know is that over-bathing leads to skin irritations and infections. Washing too often can result in dry, cracked skin, increasing the likelihood of bacteria entering the body and causing infection. The skin is the natural home of about 1,000 different species of bacteria. A natural balance keeps these in check, but if harmful bacteria get under your skin, you can get a nasty staph infection because of too much bathing. Once a day is plenty if you are not dirty.

Sharing personal care items - although it seems like a no-brainer, you might be surprised how many people share combs, hair brushes, toothbrushes, nail clippers, and other personal care items with family members or close friends. It does not matter how clean or safe you think a person is. All kinds of things can be transmitted from one person to another. *Play it safe, and do not do it.*

Using public urinals - when you have to go, you have to go, but if you are using a public urinal and getting splashed, keep in mind that you are getting splashed by every other guy who came before you. Experts will tell you to stand closer and aim slightly lower to avoid spraying. *Do not worry if this position makes noise. That is what you are there for.*

Using your hands to remove sweat - you probably work up a good sweat if you are an exercise buff. Do not make the mistake of wiping the sweat from your forehead or face with your hands. The gym is not the cleanest place, and the bacteria and viruses from a thousand hands most likely touched the machine you touched. Wiping your face will only place those germs where they can easily access your body. *Try to keep a small hand towel in your waistband to wipe away sweat.*

EATING FOR LIFE

Eat various foods - we need several different nutrients for good health; no single food can supply this. It is not about a single meal. It is about a balanced food choice that will make a difference over time! A low-fat dinner could follow a high-fat lunch.

Build your diet with foods rich in carbohydrates - around half of the calories in our food must come from foods high in carbohydrates, like cereals, rice, pasta, potatoes, and bread. Including at least one of these at every meal is a good idea: wholegrain foods, like wholegrain bread, pasta, and cereals, will increase your fiber intake.

Replace saturated with unsaturated fat - fats are essential for good health and proper body functioning. Still, too much of it can adversely affect body weight and cardiovascular health. Different types of fats have different health effects, and a few of these tips could help keep the balance right:

- Restrict consumption of total and saturated fats (frequently coming from foods of animal origin) and avoid trans fats altogether. Reading labels will help to identify the sources.

- Remove the meat's fatty parts when cooking, boiling, steaming, or baking. Use vegetable oils rather than frying.

- Eat fish 2-3 times a week, and at least a serving of oily fish will contribute to our proper intake of unsaturated fats.

Enjoy plenty of fruits and vegetables - they are essential for providing vitamins, minerals, and fiber. We should try to eat at least five servings a day. For example, at breakfast, a glass of fresh fruit juice, perhaps an apple or a slice of watermelon, and a good portion of different vegetables at each meal.

Reduce your salt and sugar intake - high-salt consumption will cause high blood pressure and an increased risk of cardiovascular disease. The following are some different ways to reduce salt in your diet:

- When shopping, choose products with low sodium content.

- When cooking, substituting spices for salt adds to flavor and taste.

- When you eat, it helps not to have salt at the table and not to add salt before tasting the food.

Sugar provides sweetness and a pleasant taste. But sugary foods and drinks are energy-rich and must be enjoyed as an occasional treat. You might use fruit instead, even to sweeten your foods and beverages.

Eat regularly and control portion sizes - consuming a variety of foods regularly and in a healthy amount is the best formula for a healthy diet. Avoiding meals, especially breakfast, can lead to out-of-control hunger, often leading to helpless overeating. Snacking between meals can help control your appetite, but snacking should not replace proper meals. You could select yogurt, a handful of fresh or dry fruits or vegetables, unsalted nuts, or bread with some cheese for snacks.

Pay attention to portion size. It helps you not to consume too many calories and allows you to eat the foods you enjoy without eliminating any!

- Cooking the right amount makes it easier not to overeat.

- Some reasonable serving sizes are 100 g of meat, a medium piece of fruit, and half a cup of raw pasta.

- Using smaller plates helps with smaller servings.

- Packaged food products, with calorie values on the package, may aid in portion sizes.

- If eating out, you could share a portion with a friend.

Drink plenty of fluids - adults must drink at least 1.5 liters daily, or more if it is hot or you are physically active. Water is the best source; tap, mineral, sparkling, non-sparkling, plain, or flavored water. Fruit juice, tea, soft drinks, milk, or other substitutes can all be acceptable occasionally.

Maintain a healthy body weight - the correct weight depends on gender, height, age, and genes. Obesity and overweight increase the risks of various diseases, including diabetes, heart disease, and cancer. Surplus body fat comes from eating more than we need. Excess calories can come from any caloric nutrient: protein, fat, carbohydrate, or alcohol. Fat is the most concentrated energy source, and physical activity helps us spend energy and feel good. The message is simple: when we gain weight, we must eat less and be more active!

Move And Make It A Habit!

Physical activity is vital for people of all weight ranges and health conditions. It helps us burn extra calories and is suitable for the heart and circulatory systems. It maintains or increases our muscle mass, helps us focus, and improves overall health. You need not be an athlete to get on the move; it can quickly become part of your daily routine. You can:

- Go for a walk during lunch breaks
- Make time for a family weekend activity
- Take the stairs rather than the elevator

CANCER-CAUSING FOODS

With so many people being diagnosed with cancer, perhaps it is time to see what is in our foods that could be causing these massive numbers of new cancer cases. The following is a list of foods you most likely consume that may contain carcinogens or are suspected of causing cancer.

Soda - research published in the **American Journal of Nutrition** discovered that people who consumed more than one soda per day had a greater risk of stroke than individuals who did not drink sodas. **Soda, loaded with sugar, is an empty source of calories that only causes weight gain and contribute to the nationwide epidemic of obesity.** *Consuming large amounts of this rapidly digested sugar causes your blood sugar to spike, leading to inflammation and insulin resistance.* Soda is often the root cause of **gastroesophageal reflux disease,** when the stomach contents leak into the esophagus, causing pain and the burning of the esophagus from stomach acid.

While sodas are not a direct cause of ulcers, they are well known to irritate and make those with ulcers have more pain. Sodas include artificial colorings and food chemicals like the derivative 4-methylimidazole (4-MI). It has been proven to cause cancer.

Another significant ingredient in sodas is phosphoric acid, which keeps your body from absorbing calcium. *Without calcium, your body cannot build bone, leading to osteoporosis, especially in women.*

Canned tomatoes - while fresh tomatoes are considered cancer-fighting food, canned ones are nothing like that. Most canned food containers are of concern because of what the can is lined with. Almost all canned food containers are coated with a chemical called bisphenol A, or BPA. The FDA agrees that BPA is a problem and supports efforts to either replace or, at the very least, minimize the amounts found in canned foods.

Tomatoes are considered exceptionally dangerous due to their high acidity, which causes BPA to leech from the can lining into the tomatoes. **The level of BPA may be so high that you should seriously consider not feeding the product to children.** Due to FDA law, there are no standards for labeling BPA. **So, because a can does not state it, this does not mean it does not contain BPA.** Be safe and avoid cans. Cook fresh or buy bottled glass products.

Farmed salmon - sounds like healthy food, but farm-raised salmon should be avoided. Sadly, more than 60 percent of the salmon consumed in the USA is farm raised. These fish are fed unnatural diets contaminated by chemical substances, antibiotics, pesticides, and other known carcinogens. The fish live in very crowded conditions, which results in their having 30 times the number of sea lice than wild salmon. Farmed salmon are fed chemicals to give their flesh that reddish pink color that should occur naturally but does not, resulting from a steady diet of chicken litter fed.

Furthermore, due to their diet, they have less of the healthy omega-3 we believe we are getting when we consume fish. Research has also shown that farmed salmon contain high PCBs, mercury, and cancer-causing dioxins. Avoid farmed salmon and seek labels stating you are buying **wild sockeye salmon.**

Processed meats - what exactly is processed meat? This long list of products includes but is not limited to sausages, hot dogs, bacon, and lunch meats like bologna or pimento loaf. Researchers state that excessive salts and chemicals in processed meats will damage health. **Processed meat products include numerous chemicals, preservatives, and sodium nitrates.**

Smoking meat is particularly bad as the meat picks up tar from the smoking process, the same deadly ingredient that cigarette smoke contains.

NOTE	Sodium nitrates make the meat look appealing and fresh, but they are well-known carcinogens.

Microwave popcorn - those little popcorn bags are so convenient to stick in the microwave, and most people would not think they could harm your health. Research shows that *microwave popcorn bags are lined with a chemical called perfluorooctanoic acid (PFOA).* It is a toxin also found in Teflon and is linked to infertility in women.

Research shows that exposure to PFOAs significantly increases your risk of kidney, bladder, liver, pancreas, and testicular cancers. Even though each manufacturer uses slightly different ingredients, most use soybean oil (a GMO product) and various preservatives. One is propyl gallate, a chemical that causes stomach problems and skin rashes. They do not state they are using GMO corn kernels on the label, but that is because the government says they do not have to.

Last is that **butter flavor,** produced by a chemical called diacetyl, is so toxic that one popcorn brand removed it because it was making their plant workers seriously ill. *The chemical is a known carcinogen.*

Potato chips - we know potato chips are cheap, great tasting, and a quick snack. However, their adverse effects on the body may not be worth the pleasure you derive from these crispy snacks. Potato chips are very high in fat and calories, bringing on significant weight gain. A research study in the New England Journal of Medicine found that eating just one potato chip daily caused an average 2-pound increase in one year. In addition to being full of trans-fats that lead to high cholesterol in most people, they have excessive sodium levels. For most people, this causes hypertension.

Potato chips have artificial flavors, many preservatives, and colors your body does not need. Potato chips are fried at a high temperature to make them crispy, which also causes them to make a material called acrylamide. This known carcinogen is also in cigarettes.

Hydrogenated oils - are oils removed from their vegetable source and changed chemically. The oils are frequently deodorized and colored to look appealing. All vegetable oils contain high levels of Omega 6 fatty acids. Excess Omega 6 fatty acids cause health problems, such as heart disease and cancers, especially skin cancer. A balance of Omega 3 and Omega 6 is essential. Try and get plenty of Omega 3 every day. It can be in the form of supplements and grass-fed meats. Additionally, fatty fish such as salmon and mackerel are excellent sources.

Hydrogenated oils help to preserve processed foods and to keep them looking appealing for as long as possible. *They are linked to cancer and influence cell membranes' structure and flexibility.*

Highly salted, pickled, or smoked foods - foods cured using nitrates or nitrites act as preservatives and add color to the meat. Though nitrates do not cause cancer, under certain conditions, these chemicals change once consumed into N-nitroso composites. *N-nitroso is associated with a more substantial increase in the risk of developing cancers.*

Smoking food like meat or nuts causes these items to absorb considerable amounts of tar produced by the smoke. **Tar is a known carcinogen.** Meats like bacon, sausage, bologna, and salami are high in fat and salt. Pickled foods are also very high in salt.

There is overwhelming evidence that eating these foods increases the risk of colorectal cancer and high rates of stomach cancer. Rates of stomach cancer are significant in places like Japan, where a traditional diet contains many highly salted foods and smoked foods.

Highly processed white flour - most people have heard that white flour is bad for you. You most likely have no idea how bad it is for your health. Refinery grains destroy their natural nutrients. Mills are no longer content waiting for their flour to whiten with time, so they bleach it with chlorine gas.

The EPA states chlorine gas is a dangerous irritant that is unsafe to inhale and, in large quantities, can be lethal. White powder lurks in many processed foods. *It has a very high glycemic rate, quickly raising blood sugar and insulin levels, which can directly cause diabetes. It is believed to spread cancer cells by feeding the cells directly.*

Cancerous tumors feed primarily on sugars in your bloodstream. By avoiding refined grains like white flour, you can prevent, or at the very least, starve tumors.

GMOs - genetically modified organisms, more commonly called GMOs, are foods changed by chemicals and grown with chemicals.

<table>
<tr><td>NOTE</td><td>Most American consumers believe the FDA has approved GMO foods, which is untrue. The FDA does not have any testing procedures for GMO foods!</td></tr>
</table>

Sadly, almost all grains, including soybeans, wheat, and corn, are grown via GMOs. Read labels carefully and look for brands that state the food is **GMO-free** because GMOs do not have to be listed.

Refined sugars - are known to spike insulin levels, are the preferred food for cancer cells, and promote their growth. Cancer seems to have a sweet tooth. It is a known fact that has been around for many years. Tumors and cancers use sugars to "feed" themselves and increase in size. **Cancer cells prefer to feed on fructose-rich sweeteners like high-fructose corn syrup (HFCS) to proliferate.** The reason is that HFCS is metabolized by cancer cells most quickly and easily.

<table>
<tr><td>FYI</td></tr>
<tr><td>The reader should understand why high-fructose corn syrup is considered the worst offender. And given that cakes, pies, cookies, sodas, juices, sauces, cereals, and many other popular, processed food items are laden with refined sugars and HFCS. This should explain why cancer rates are on the rise.</td></tr>
</table>

Artificial sweetener - most people use artificial sweeteners to lose weight or because they have diabetes and must avoid sugar. The main problem is that numerous studies show that people who regularly consume artificial sweeteners, such as sodas or coffee sweeteners, gain weight. It also has little or nothing to help those with diabetes.

Artificial sweeteners make it even more challenging to control blood sugar levels and worsen conditions related to diabetes, such as cataracts and gastroparesis. Aspartame is found to cause convulsions, which some people will mistake for an insulin reaction. Artificial sweeteners prevent the body's ability to monitor daily calorie intake and make the body crave additional sweets.

<table>
<tr><td>NOTE</td><td>There is growing evidence that the chemicals that make up artificial sweeteners, particularly aspartame, break down in the body to a deadly toxin called DKP. When your stomach processes this chemical, it creates chemicals that can cause cancer, particularly a brain tumor.</td></tr>
</table>

Anything diet - including frozen foods, prepackaged foods, and diet sodas labeled **diet** or **low fat** generally contains aspartame, a chemical, artificial sweetener. *Studies indicate that aspartame causes many diseases and sicknesses, such as cancers, congenital disabilities, and heart problems.*

Dietary food is chemically processed and made from super-refined ingredients, excessive sodium levels, and artificial colors and flavors to make it taste good. **Remember, artificial anything is NOT real food!**

Red meat - evidence shows that red meat is good in your diet, in small, infrequent amounts. *Grass-fed beef contains conjugated linoleic acid that fights against certain cancers.*

However, in a study over ten years, eating red meat daily, even a small amount, such as that quarter-pound hamburger, increases a man's risk of death from cancer by 22 percent and a woman's chance by 20 percent. *Other studies have shown that eating much red meat increases the risk of breast, prostate, and colon cancer.*

NOTE	Red meat is especially dangerous when talking about colon cancer. Studies have shown that long-term consumption of red meat significantly increases the amount of colon cancer found in the subjects studied. On the other hand, the long-term consumption of fish and poultry appeared to be protective.

Non-organic fruits - are contaminated with hazardous pesticides such as atrazine, thiodicarb, organophosphates, and high-nitrogen fertilizers.

Atrazine is banned in European countries but is still used in the U.S. It is a weed killer that causes severe human problems, particularly in our reproductive capabilities.

Traditional foods are also subjected to an enormous amount of chemicals and hormones to make the fruit and veggies grow more prominent. Apples are undoubtedly the worst offenders, with pesticides showing on more than 98 percent of all apples tested. Fruits with a 90 percent positive rate of pesticide residue included oranges, strawberries, and grapes. Washing fruit does not remove 100 percent of the pesticide residue.

Pesticides are toxic to insects as well as human beings.

FOODS TO AVOID

Everyone knows the healthy foods and those that are not, right? Yet, many foods on store shelves are still advertised as **healthy options** but are far from a decent choice. A few of the worst offenders are loaded with ingredients that, besides being unhealthy, will keep those inches on your waistline. Then there are still other healthy foods that are too dangerous to consider eating.

Many foods would make this list, and it might be hard to avoid them. Here we are presenting some of the most frequently purchased offenders. **Remove them from your diet if you care about your health.**

Stick margarine - though long touted as the healthier alternative to butter, this is another falsehood. Stick margarine contains excessive amounts of trans-fats that damage your blood vessels and arteries and has numerous calories. At least 100 calories per tablespoon!

Previously, it was believed that, by avoiding animal fats, margarine was a healthier choice. But, over the years, researchers have discovered that natural butter from organic, grass-fed cows is better for your body rather than subjecting your body to the trans-fat, salt, and artificial colors and flavors margarine has. Besides tasting great, butter is an excellent source of those healthy saturated fats, fat-soluble vitamins, and other vitamins. They sell unsalted butter if you are concerned about the calories or salt content.

You can also try using whipped butter sold in tub containers. Whipped butter has more air, hence less fat and fewer calories.

Pancakes from a mix - are an excellent breakfast choice on any morning. Americans love pancakes so much that there is even a National Pancake Day! However, you might be surprised by what is in your boxed pancake mix.

The pancake mix seems harmless enough, so much so that you may not even realize it contains trans-fats because it is a powder. If you read the labels, most pancake mixes include partially hydrogenated soybean (GMO) or cottonseed oil. If you continue reading, you will find that it also contains preservatives and salt. Ditch those artery-clogging trans-fats and GMOs, and mix your pancakes. Cooking from scratch is cheaper. You will know what is in the pancakes you made for your family. And it is just as easy as the box mix and much healthier.

Tomato sauce - in itself, tomatoes are very good for you, as they are laden with vitamin C, iron, and vitamin A. While it may seem easy to get a can or bottle of tomato sauce for a pasta dinner, what is in that container might surprise you.

Commercially produced tomato sauce is laden with refined sugars. Read the label! A few brands list corn syrup as the second ingredient, but more than likely, you already have too much sugar in your diet. You do not need it in your tomato sauce. Many tomato sauces also contain sodium.

Frosting - in cans or packaged, frosting is a mixture of trans-fats, corn syrup, preservatives, artificial flavors, and artificial colors. Many of these ingredients are banned in most countries. Read the labels. Many of them state they include soybean (GMO) or cottonseed oil, and some contain two different types of sugar. One label says "sugar" as the main ingredient, which is more than likely from GMO sugar beets, and then high maltose corn syrup, aka high fructose corn syrup. Interestingly, even the frosting that states its flavor is vanilla, so it should be white but has artificial colors.

Packaged sandwiches - whenever you are rushed for lunch, you may think picking up a premade sandwich is healthier than fast food. But you would be making a mistake. Though convenient, ready-made sandwiches are not worth the money or the health problems. The average sandwich has more than 400 calories and is made with white bread, essentially empty calories.

Although you probably already know that mayonnaise is unhealthy, you might not know that just one tablespoon has 11 grams of fat. Most prepackaged sandwiches come with at least four tablespoons. If your sandwich includes cheese (usually American cheese or with a cheese product), just one ounce contains more than 10 grams of fat.

Most sandwiches use the unhealthiest type of meat you can use, such as bologna or salami. These lunchmeats use the animals' leftover parts, such as the heart, intestines, and stomach.

Non-organic strawberries - seem clean and pure, but did you ever seen workers in a strawberry field? They have to wear protective suits when working to avoid being exposed to the dozens of pesticides sprayed on strawberries regularly. A U.S. Department of Agriculture report discovered that strawberries contained more than 13 pesticides. You may have heard that the EPA forbids using the pesticide methyl iodide because it is a known carcinogen. However, that does not mean there are not a multitude of other pesticides being used.

Although California is leading the way in investigating non-toxic, or at least a less toxic, means of controlling insects and fungi, you need to know that these are small-scale studies. Almost all these juicy fruits are still sprayed with highly toxic chemicals, and the pesticides are absorbed into the strawberries. So washing them does not work! *Be safe, and only buy organic strawberries.*

Coleslaw - contains cabbage and carrots, which are very good for you but loaded with calories, sugars, and a tremendous amount of fat. The fat comes from the mayonnaise.

Sprouts - the problem is that they have been a part of so many recalls due to health issues that it is hard to track them all. Over the last 20 years, there have been more than 40 recalls owing to contamination, and it does not matter which kind of sprout, bean, alfalfa, or pea.

The thing that makes sprouts grow, warm moist conditions, are also ideal for making bacteria such as salmonella, E. coli, and listeria grow. Also, when you buy sprouts from a store, you have no idea how old they are, and sprouts can grow dangerous bacteria in a matter of days if not appropriately handled.

Packaged cookies - another no-brainer, cookies are not healthy. It is common knowledge. Check the label to see if it is made with partially hydrogenated cooking oil. If they are, put them back. If you read the label, they will have white flour, lots of sugar, artificial flavors, colors, and preservatives. *If you must indulge, look for cookies with "high oleic" oils. They keep the product fresher without all the trans-fats.*

Frozen pizza - you know pizza is not the best food choice, but do you know just one slice of commercially made pizza contains one full day's worth of salt? Of course, it depends on the toppings and crust, but almost everything in pizza has salt and MSG, including the dough and cheese. If your pizza includes processed meats such as sausage or pepperoni, you get a lot of nitrates and salt intake. Pizza is also unbelievably high in fat. Most come from cheese, but many pizza sauces contain palm oil, corn, and sugar.

Did you know that depending on your toppings, just one slice of a deep-dish pizza has approximately 400 to 500 calories? And as much as 30 grams of fat per slice.

Salty snacks - remember the famous potato chip commercial that touted "Betcha can't eat just one?" Talk about meaningless calories! In addition to the high salt content, almost all salty snacks are fried in partially hydrogenated oils (again, read GMO oil), which makes them loaded with trans-fats. Read the labels, and you will find that these foods use artificial flavors, seasonings, and colors to make them more appealing. *However, the damage to your heart and arteries is NOT appealing.*

Ketchup - the second most prominent ingredient in ketchup is high fructose corn syrup (sugar). That means that it is GMO corn. A few labels even state that their ketchup has two different kinds of sugar! Mixing sugar and fats (ketchup on your fries) is dangerous for your health. Additionally, the ketchup is usually listed as being from concentrate, which means it has been heated and boiled down, removing most of the nutrients which would have given it health benefits.

Numerous brands of ketchup also contain excessive sodium levels, artificial colors, artificial flavors, and many preservatives. The majority of these things are just not good for your body. *If you love ketchup, look for ketchup low or no sugar added and keep your consumption to a minimum.*

Packaged cereals - today, cereals are laden with everything you try to avoid. Sugar is the first one. Some cereals list sugar as their second ingredient! Right behind that GMO corn they are using.

Also, all those little shapes like puffs, stars, or O's are made by an extruder. It mixes the grains with water and then, at a high temperature, shoots them out of little holes into those shapes. Nearly all nutrients are cooked out of the grains during this process. *You should also note that all cereals contain artificial colors, flavors, and vast amounts of preservatives.*

Ranch dressing - although it tastes great, it is unsuitable for your health. Each tablespoon contains more than 75 calories. What many consider a typical serving (at least an ounce) has 137 calories and more than 7 grams of fat! Most people consume approximately 100 grams on an average salad. 100 grams are almost 500 calories!

Ranch dressing is also **laden with sugar, modified food starch, artificial flavors, artificial colors, and malt dextrin,** all things you do not need in your body. *Ranch dressing may* *taste good, but it is not worth damaging your health or ruining your diet.*

Mechanically produced hamburgers - when you see those packages of industrially produced hamburgers, think of this: Crowded cattle raised in filthy stalls pumped with antibiotics and hormones, eating revolting diets at best. Your single hamburger patty does not come from just one animal but combines hundreds of cows. That means there is a more considerable risk of E. coli contamination. This ground beef also contains something you may have heard of called pink slime. Pink slime is the fat that the slaughterhouse cuts off the meat. Formerly sold only as dog food, this pink slime is now doused in ammonia, then ground up with the meat as filler.

The USDA does not think this pink slime needs to be labeled since, in their logic, it is part of the cow. Therefore, in their minds, it is beef. Be safe and eat healthy. Eat only grass-fed beef.

FLATULENCE

Passing gas or farting. No matter what you call it, everyone does it. On some days, people fart more than others. And on other days, farts are smellier, and those days can be embarrassing. But what causes the smell to change?

Where Do Farts Come From?

Flatus and flatulence are the medical words for farts and farting. Farts consist of common gases like hydrogen, methane, and carbon dioxide. These gases are not toxic and are in the air you breathe.

Gasses enter the gastrointestinal (GI) tract in three different ways:

Swallowing air - the air is sucked into the lungs when inhaled, but some also enters the stomach. Eating and drinking too quickly, chewing gum or tobacco, and drinking fizzy beverages can increase the amount of air that enters the stomach.

Creation of gas by bacteria in the colon - healthy bacteria (normal gut flora) live in the colon and help digest food. The digestion process produces gases. Certain foods are harder to digest than others. And some create foul-smelling gases when broken down.

Movement of air from the bloodstream to the bowel - a very tiny amount of air moves from the blood into the bowels. The amount is so tiny that it almost does not count.

What Causes Farts To Smell Bad?

Most farts do not smell. That is because hydrogen, methane, and carbon dioxide, the primary gasses that makeup farts, do not have odors. But everyone's gut flora is different. Some people have smellier farts than others.

What about farts that are so foul-smelling that they clear out the room? Something different in the gut adds to the foul odor in these cases. It is typically from something you ate. In rare cases, a medication or medical condition can cause the stink.

Causes of really foul farts include:

- Diet

- Lactose intolerance (inability to properly digest foods with lactose, like cow's milk)

- Medications (especially antibiotics)

- Constipation (a traffic jam of extra stool can add odor to gas as it is passed)

- Colorectal cancer (this is less likely without other concerning symptoms)

Some conditions can also cause stinky farts, and diarrhea often happens along with these conditions:

- Celiac disease (allergy to gluten)

- Small intestinal bacterial overgrowth (SIBO), or too much bacteria in the GI tract

- Giardia infection (a common parasite)

How Can You Get Rid Of Smelly Farts?
Generally speaking, stinky farts will go away once the cause has worked its way out of your system. ***To help prevent smelly farts in the future, consider making some changes to your diet.***

The following foods increase the amount of gas and smelliness of farts:

- Artificial sweeteners in sugar-free foods (like xylitol and sorbitol)

- Beans, lentils, and bean-based products (like hummus, tofu, and tempeh)

- Beer

- Certain fruits (like prunes and apricots)

- Certain vegetables (like brussel sprouts, broccoli, cabbage, and cauliflower)

- Dairy products from cow's milk (if you have a lactose intolerance)

- Fatty, fried foods

- Foods high in fiber (like whole grains)

- High-protein foods (like animal meat) and powders (commonly used to build muscle)

When something other than food causes smelly farts, the objective is to treat the underlying cause. For example, if your provider finds you have small intestinal bacterial overgrowth (SIBO), they will recommend antibiotic treatment. You can treat lactose intolerance by avoiding dairy and taking lactase supplements to help the gut digest milk products. And if constipation is the problem, there are ways to deal with that, too.

Medications To Decrease Farting Or Stinky Farts?
Unfortunately, no. Though it might be nice to eliminate farts, farting is just a part of life. Most people pass gas about 10 to 20 times per day.

Studies have shown that simethicone (GasX), activated charcoal, and alpha-galactosidase (Beano) are ineffective. Interestingly, there are odor-reducing products such as underwear made from activated carbon fiber fabric or charcoal pads you wear inside of underwear. They might help, but these are not widely available.

Are Smelly Farts Or Too Many Farts A Bad Sign?
Lots of gas or foul smelly gas can be embarrassing. Fortunately, it is rarely a sign of a serious medical problem. When it comes to smelly farts or lots of farts, diet is most likely the culprit. But some symptoms could raise concern for a more significant issue.

Talk to your provider if you experience any of the following concerning symptoms:

- Bloody stools or dark black, tar-colored stools
- Fevers
- Severe abdominal tenderness

- Severe diarrhea
- Severe vomiting
- Unintentional weight loss or loss of appetite

Your provider may ask you more questions, examine you, and possibly order tests. Together you can devise a plan to figure out what is going on.

ALLERGIES

Allergies ensue when the immune system responds to a foreign substance, like pollen, bee venom, pet dander, or food, which does not cause a reaction in most people. The immune system creates substances known as antibodies. When you have allergies, the immune system creates antibodies that identify the allergen as harmful, even though it is not. When you encounter this allergen, the immune system's response can inflame your skin, sinuses, airways, or digestive system.

The severity of allergies varies for each person and could range from minor irritation to anaphylaxis, a potentially life-threatening emergency. While most allergies cannot be cured, treatments can help relieve your allergy symptoms.

Symptoms
Allergic symptoms depend on the substance involved and can affect airways, sinuses and nasal passages, skin, and the digestive system. The allergic response may range from mild to severe, and in some severe cases, allergies may trigger a life-threatening response identified as anaphylaxis.

Hay fever, also known as allergic rhinitis, can result in:

- Itch of the nose, eyes, or roof of the mouth
- Runny, stuffy nose
- Sneezing
- Watery, red, or swollen eyes (conjunctivitis)

A food allergy can cause:

- Anaphylaxis
- Hives
- Inflammation of the lips, tongue, face, or throat
- Tingling in the mouth

Insects bite allergies could cause:

- Large areas of swelling (edema) at the sting site
- Itching or hives all over the body
- Cough, chest tightness, wheezing, or shortness of breath
- Anaphylaxis

A drug allergy can cause:

- Anaphylaxis
- Facial swelling
- Hives
- Itchy skin
- Rash
- Wheezing

Allergic dermatitis, an allergic skin condition also called eczema, can cause the skin to:

- Anaphylaxis
- Flake or peel
- Itch
- Redden

Certain types of allergies, including allergies to foods and insect stings, can lead to a severe reaction known simply as anaphylaxis. In a life-threatening medical emergency, anaphylaxis may cause you to go into shock.

Signs and symptoms of anaphylaxis include:

- A drop in blood pressure
- A rapid, weak pulse
- Lightheadedness
- Loss of consciousness
- Nausea and vomiting

- Severe shortness of breath
- Skin rash

When You Should See Your Provider

Contact your health care provider if you experience symptoms you believe are caused by an allergy and nonprescription allergy medications do not provide relief. Call the provider who prescribed it immediately if you are experiencing symptoms after starting a new medication.

For intense allergic reactions (anaphylaxis), call 911 or your local emergency number to seek emergency medical help. If you own an epinephrine auto-injector (Auvi-Q, EpiPen, or other), give yourself a shot immediately. Even if symptoms improve after the epinephrine injection, **you must go to the emergency department to ensure symptoms do not return when the effects of the injection wear off.**

If you have had a severe allergy attack or any signs and symptoms of anaphylaxis, make an appointment with your physician. Assessment, diagnosis, and long-term management of anaphylaxis are complicated, so you must see a specialist in allergies and immunology.

Causes

Allergic reactions begin when the immune system mistakes a harmless substance for a dangerous invader. The immune function then produces antibodies that remain alert for that particular allergen. If exposed to the allergen again, these antibodies can release several immune function chemicals, such as histamine, initiating allergic reactions.

Frequent allergy triggers include:

- Air-borne allergens, such as pollen, animal dander, dust mites, and mold

- Insect stings, like from a bee or wasp

- Latex or other substances you touch can cause allergic skin reactions.

- Medications, particularly penicillin or penicillin-based antibiotics

- Some foods, particularly peanuts, tree nuts, wheat, soy, fish, shellfish, eggs, and milk

Risk factors
You could be more likely to develop an allergy if you:

- Are a child

- Have a family history of asthma or allergies, like hay fever, hives, or eczema

- Have asthma or another allergic condition

Complications
Getting an allergy increases your risk of having other medical issues, including:

Anaphylaxis - if you have severe allergies, you are at an increased risk of this severe allergy-induced reaction. Foods, medications, and insect stings are among the most common triggers of anaphylaxis.

Asthma - if you have an allergy, you probably have asthma, the immune system reaction that affects the airways and breathing. In many instances, asthma could be caused by exposure to an allergen in the environment (allergy-induced asthma).

Sinusitis and infections of the ears or lungs - the risk of acquiring these conditions is greater if you have hay fever or asthma.

Prevention
Preventing an allergic reaction depends on the type of allergy you have. General measures include the following:

Avoid known triggers - even if you are treating your allergy symptoms, try to avoid triggers. If allergic to pollen, stay indoors with windows and doors closed when pollen is high. If allergic to dust mites, dust, vacuum and wash your bedding frequently.

Keep a diary - when you try to identify what causes or worsens your allergy symptoms, monitor your activities, what you eat when symptoms occur, and what seems to help. It may help you and your provider identify triggers.

Wearing a medical alert bracelet - wearing a medical alert bracelet (or necklace) will let others know you have a severe allergy if you have a reaction and cannot communicate.

ALLERGY MEDICATIONS

Allergy medicines are available in **tablets, liquids, inhalers, nasal sprays, eyedrops, skin creams, and shots (injections).** Several are over-the-counter (OTC); others are available by prescription only.

The following summarizes the types of allergy medications and why they are used:

Antihistamines
Antihistamines block histamine, the symptom-causing chemical released by the body's immune system during an allergic reaction.

Pills and liquids - oral antihistamines are available over-the-counter and by prescription. They ease a runny nose, itchy or watery eyes, hives, swelling, and other signs or symptoms of allergies. Because some drugs can make you feel drowsy and tired, take them cautiously when driving or doing other activities requiring alertness.

Antihistamines that tend to cause drowsiness include:

- Chlorpheniramine
- Diphenhydramine

The following antihistamines are less likely to initiate sleepiness:

- Cetirizine (Zyrtec, Zyrtec Allergy)
- Desloratadine (Clarinex)
- Fexofenadine (Allegra, Allegra Allergy)
- Levocetirizine (Xyzal, Xyzal Allergy)
- Loratadine (Alavert, Claritin)

Nasal sprays - antihistamine nasal sprays help to reduce sneezes, itchy or runny nose, sinus congestion, and postnasal drip. Secondary effects of antihistamine nasal sprays might include a bitter taste, drowsiness, or tiredness. Prescription antihistamine nasal sprays include:

- Azelastine (Astelin, Astepro)
- Olopatadine (Patanase)

Eyedrops - antihistamine eyedrops are available over-the-counter or by prescription. They can ease itchy, red, and swollen eyes. These drops could have a combination of antihistamines and other medicines.

Side effects might include headaches and dry eyes. If antihistamine drops sting or burn, keep them in the refrigerator or use refrigerated artificial tear drops before you use them. Examples include:

- Ketotifen (Alaway, Zaditor)
- Olopatadine (Pataday, Patanol, Pazeo)
- Pheniramine and naphazoline (Visine, Opcon-A, others)

Decongestants

They are used for quick, temporary relief of nasal and sinus congestion. They may cause trouble sleeping, headache, increased blood pressure, and irritability. They are not recommended for individuals with high blood pressure, cardiovascular disease, glaucoma, or hyperthyroidism.

Pills and liquids - oral decongestants relieve nasal and sinus congestion caused by hay fever (allergic rhinitis). Many decongestants, such as pseudoephedrine (Sudafed), are available over-the-counter.

Several oral allergy medications contain a decongestant and an antihistamine. Examples include:

- Cetirizine and pseudoephedrine (Zyrtec-D 12 Hour)
- Desloratadine and pseudoephedrine (Clarinex-D)
- Fexofenadine and pseudoephedrine (Allegra-D)
- Loratadine and pseudoephedrine (Claritin-D)

Nasal spray and drops - alleviate nasal and sinus congestion when used only for a short time. Repeated use for over three consecutive days can lead to a cycle where congestion recurs or worsens. Examples are:

- Oxymetazoline (Afrin)
- Tetrahydrozoline (Tyzine)

Corticosteroids
Corticosteroids alleviate symptoms by blocking allergies-related inflammation.

Nasal sprays - corticosteroid sprays prevent and alleviate stuffiness, sneezing, and runny nose. Side effects may include an unpleasant taste, nasal irritation, and nosebleeds. Examples include:

- Budesonide (Rhinocort)
- Fluticasone furoate (Flonase Sensimist)
- Fluticasone propionate (Flonase Allergy Relief)
- Mometasone (Nasonex)
- Triamcinolone (Nasacort Allergy 24 Hour)

For people bothered by the feeling of liquid running down their throats or with the unpleasant taste of these sprays, there are two aerosol formulas:

- Beclomethasone (Qnasl)
- Ciclesonide (Zetonna)

Inhalers - are commonly used as part of the asthma treatment caused or complicated by reactions to airborne allergy triggers (allergens). Side effects can include mouth and throat irritation and oral yeast infections and are generally minor.

Some inhalers combine corticosteroids with long-acting bronchodilators. Prescription inhalers include:

- Beclomethasone (Qvar Redihaler)
- Budesonide (Pulmicort Flexhaler)
- Ciclesonide (Alvesco)
- Fluticasone (Flovent)
- Mometasone (Asmanex Twisthaler)

Eyedrops - are used to alleviate persistent itchy, red, or watery eyes when other interventions are ineffective. A medical doctor specializing in eye disorders (ophthalmologist) usually monitors such drops because of cataracts, glaucoma, and infection risk. Examples include:

- Fluorometholone (Flarex, FML)
- Loteprednol (Alrex, Lotemax)
- Prednisolone (Omnipred, Pred Forte, others)

Pills and liquids - are used for treating symptoms caused by allergic reactions. Long-term use can cause cataracts, osteoporosis, muscle weakness, stomach ulcers, increased blood sugar (glucose), and delayed growth in children. Oral corticosteroids can worsen high blood pressure.

Prescription oral corticosteroids include:

- Prednisolone (Prelone)
- Prednisone (Prednisone Intensol, Rayos)
- Methylprednisolone (Medrol)

Skin creams - alleviate allergic skin reactions such as itching, redness, or scaling. Low-potency corticosteroid creams are available without a prescription. Talk to your doctor before using these drugs for more than a few weeks.

Side effects may include skin discoloration and irritation. Long-term use, especially of more potent prescription corticosteroids, can cause skin thinning and abnormal hormone levels. Examples include:

- Betamethasone (Dermabet, Diprolene, others)
- Desonide (Desonate, DesOwen)
- Hydrocortisone (Locoid, Micort-HC, others)
- Mometasone (Elocon)
- Triamcinolone

Mast Cell Stabilizers

Blocks the release of chemicals in the immune system that contribute to allergic reactions. These drugs are generally safe and must be used for several days to produce the full effect. They are used when antihistamines do not work or are not tolerated.

Nasal spray - over-the-counter nasal sprays include cromolyn (Nasalcrom).

Eyedrops - prescription eyedrops include the following:

- Cromolyn (Crolom)
- Lodoxamide (Alomide)
- Nedocromil (Alocril)

Leukotriene Inhibitors

Are prescription medications that block the symptom-causing chemicals called leukotrienes. The oral medication alleviates allergy signs and symptoms, including nasal congestion, runny nose, and sneezing. Only one type of this drug, montelukast (Singulair), has been approved for treating hay fever.

In some people, leukotriene inhibitors might cause psychological symptoms like anxiety, depression, strange dreams, trouble sleeping, and suicidal thinking or behavior.

Allergen Immunotherapy

When carefully timed, exposure is increased gradually to allergens, particularly those difficult to avoid, such as pollens, dust mites, and molds. The goal is to train the body's immune system not to react to allergens. Immunotherapy can be used when other treatments are not effective or tolerated. It is also helpful in reducing asthma symptoms in some patients.

Shots - may be given as a series of injections, usually once or twice a week. The dose can be increased weekly or every two weeks based on the individual's tolerance. Injections of the maximum tolerated dose may be given year-round every two to four weeks.
Side effects can include irritation at the injection site and allergy symptoms such as sneezing, congestion, or hives. Infrequently allergy shots can cause anaphylaxis, an abrupt life-threatening reaction that causes swelling in the throat, difficulty breathing, and other signs and symptoms.

Sublingual immunotherapy (SLIT) - with this immunotherapy, an allergen-based tablet is placed under the tongue (sublingual) and allowed to be absorbed. This treatment has been shown to reduce runny nose, congestion, eye irritation, and other symptoms associated with hay fever. It also improves asthma symptoms.

One SLIT tablet contains dust mites (Odactra). Several SLIT tablets contain extracts from pollens of different types of grass, including the following:

- Short ragweed (Ragwitek)
- Sweet vernal, orchard, perennial rye, Timothy, and Kentucky blue grass (Oralair)
- Timothy grass (Grastek)

Biological medications - some medicines target a specific reaction in the immune system and try to prevent it from happening. These medicines are given as injections. They include dupilumab (Dupixent) to treat allergic skin reactions and omalizumab (Xolair) to treat asthma or hives when other medications do not help.

Side effects of biological medications may include redness, itchiness, irritation of the eyes, and irritation at the injection site.

Emergency Epinephrine Shots
They are used to treat anaphylaxis, a sudden, life-threatening reaction. The drug is administered with a self-injecting syringe and needle device (auto-injector). You might need to carry two auto-injectors if there is a chance you could have a severe allergic reaction to a particular food, such as peanuts, or if you are allergic to bee or wasp venom.

A second injection is sometimes needed. As a result, it is crucial to call 911 or get immediate emergency medical care.

A health care professional will train you to use an epinephrine auto-injector. It is vital to get the type that your doctor prescribes, as the method for injection may differ slightly for each brand. Also, be sure to replace your emergency epinephrine before the expiration date.

Examples of these medications include:

- Adrenaclick
- Auvi-Q
- EpiPen
- EpiPen Jr

Get Your Doctor's Advice

Work with your doctor to choose the most effective allergy medications and avoid problems. Even over-the-counter allergy medications have side effects. Some can cause problems when combined with other medications.

It is crucial to talk to your doctor about taking allergy medications in the following circumstances:

- You are pregnant or breastfeeding.

- You have a chronic health condition, such as diabetes, glaucoma, osteoporosis, or high blood pressure.

- You are taking other medications, including herbal supplements.

- You are treating allergies in a child. Children need different doses of medication or other medications from adults.

- You are treating allergies in an older adult. Some allergy medications can cause confusion, urinary tract symptoms, or other side effects in older adults.

- You are already taking an allergy medication that is not working. Bring the medication with you in its original bottle or package when you see your doctor.

Keep track of your symptoms, when you use your medications, and how much you use them. It will help your doctor figure out what works best. You might need to try a few medications to determine which are most effective and have the least bothersome side effects.

LIFE SKILLS

Essential Life Skills To Be An Adult

In theory, all adults know that they should be ready for anything. But mostly, we feel unequipped to handle all the curves that life throws at us. **Sometimes it is HARD to be a grownup!**

So, What Is A Life Skill?

It is a skill that is necessary or desirable for participation in everyday life. Life skills include:

Housekeeping Skills

Basic housekeeping skills and how to clean - from making your bed to the laundry basics, we all need basic housekeeping skills. Boys and girls, from high school students to grandparents, know that maintaining a tidy house is a life skill that safeguards health, keeps you organized, allows you to find what you need, and generally saves you money to keep living.

How to cook - not all of us are gourmet chefs. If you are not a big kitchen fan, have a few low-effort dishes you feel confident whipping up. The ability to cook and enjoy a meal is a necessary life skill that will save you money and help you maintain your health.

Home repairs - we know DIY can help save considerable time on home repairs. When you can refrain from turning over cash whenever you have a minor household issue, it helps your bottom line. Home Depot, Lowes, and other home improvement chains offer classes and workshops to help you tackle your next home repair job.

How to unclog a toilet or sink - a life skill nobody wants, but if you have ever clogged a toilet or walked into an overflowing bathroom, you will be grateful to know how to wield a plunger. There are several tutorials and YouTube videos on how to unclog a toilet creatively, but go with the old standby plunger when in doubt.

How you use kitchen appliances - from knowing how to clean your fridge and maintain its efficiency to understanding how to use the settings on kitchen appliances is sometimes mysterious and not often thought about. If you have anything in your kitchen you do not use or that is too complicated to use, ask yourself if it is taking up space or if it is valuable enough to invest your time to learn to take advantage of the full functionality of the appliance.

Technical Skills

How to write - not everyone needs to be able to blog or to be able to write a masterpiece, but with a basic understanding of sentence structure and written expression, it can take you far in life. Some people DISLIKE writing, while others feel it is the only way they can truly express their inner thoughts. If you are of the former, consider taking an introductory creative writing class or finding a writing course online to help you improve those skills.

How to write your resume and a cover letter - whether you are working from home or are a full-time homemaker, understanding how to write a resume and cover letter is an essential life skill. Especially if you need employment, a part-time job can help provide for your family or bridge a need gap. A creative, well-crafted resume and cover letter might help you get your foot in the door. Many employment firms, colleges, and community education centers offer resume classes, and many have staff who are happy to review your resume and give you tips.

Public speaking - like writing, speaking, especially public speaking, can cause some of us to cower in the corner. Public speaking is most likely not your favorite thing, but everyone can learn helpful tips for speaking better. The more you practice, the better you will become.

Effective communication is a vital life skill - no one makes it through the world alone, so learning to communicate with others will help you to get where you need to be in life, and it is a learned skill. It is all about expressing your needs and desires while understanding and relating to the needs and desires of others.
Communicating with your spouse, children, and friends can help you learn, grow, and become stronger. Through communication, we form relationships and friendships, so being good at it means you will be successful in your interactions with others.

Technology - basic computer skills are necessary today. At a minimum, you must be able to email and use the Internet for basic searches. Technology is a powerful and helpful tool that can simplify your life.

How to back up files - save your files and save them often. Back up your phone and computer to the cloud or an external hard drive. Nothing is more devastating than losing work hours because you did not back it up. If you are a blogger, writing posts somewhere like Google Drive or Dropbox, where the file is automatically saved every few minutes versus directly in the blog program, could save a lot of pain and frustration if a post goes awry.

Protect your passwords - your password is like a key. So, can you imagine using the same key for your car, house, and office? That would be ridiculous; using the same unprotected password for everything is equivalent.

Survival Skills

How to keep yourself safe - it is common to WANT to stay safe and avoid unsafe situations. However, we see on the news and in daily life many people who go against that logic and put themselves in dangerous situations. Not to say you should not take risks, but you must learn to take precautions in all situations.

Emergency preparedness - when a natural disaster hits, what would you do? What would happen if your home burned down or you were in an accident? Emergency preparation can appear extreme and scary, but having basic emergency skills and knowing what to do if disaster strikes can help you gain peace of mind and help keep you and your family safe. It is not too late to act today!

Basic first aid - do you know what to do if anyone has a deep cut or a broken bone? Would you know the signs of a heart attack, a stroke, or a concussion? Pick up a first aid book if you feel your skills are rusty or you do not have any. It is common to panic in emergencies, but if you are versed in first aid, you can rely on your instincts and knowledge and come to the rescue with a clear head.

How would you survive without electricity - a part of emergency preparedness, the prospect of going without electricity can be daunting and scary. The ability to unplug and entertain yourself without technology or even without the use of lights, television, and a stove is a skill, which at the very least, will get you and your family through the next power outage and, at best, will help you to communicate better and get away from your cell phones.

How to read a map - with GPS available on almost every smartphone, map reading is rapidly becoming obsolete. But aside from learning this ability for the occasional digital detox, map reading is vital, even if it is so that you can understand geography and route yourself accordingly. Anyone who attempts to navigate a subway system or spend time in a rural area with spotty data service will quickly realize the merits of being able to read a map. Refresh your map reading abilities and learn to take inventory of your location wherever you are.

Car repair - if you have a car, you should understand essential maintenance, even if it is to keep you from getting ripped off at the repair shop. Depending on where you grew up, pumping your gas might seem laughable or present a real challenge. Brush up on essential car skills to feel comfortable when behind the wheel.

Money Management Skills

How to budget - budgeting and being financially responsible are vital to your life skillset. Whether you are just starting to get a handle on your finances or are an experienced voucher-clipping, money-saving guru, understanding your budget is the first step to achieving financial peace and security. It is a skill we can learn from a very young age and should build on throughout our lives.

How to avoid or get out of debt - on debt, everyone talks a lot about financial peace and getting out of debt. Being debt-free is freedom, but it takes work. Learning to live within your means is a learned skill. Learning to slay your debt is about keeping your spending in check and managing a plan to pay off your debt quickly and efficiently.

How to make a significant purchase - maybe you are about to buy a home, car, or just your first washing machine. Whatever it is, you should understand how to compare prices, research, and make an intelligent purchase.

Balancing your bank account - may seem silly, but how many of us use debit cards without writing things down? How many of us pay bills online or have them set up to automatically debit from our accounts and then forget until they appear on bank statements? Recording your expenses is a skill that will keep you in touch with your finances. It keeps you immediately accountable for what you are spending.

How to use coupons - coupons will save you money! Yes, it is a skill that can seem daunting, but it is straightforward to get started. Most stores now offer e-coupons you can clip on your phone and scan once you are at the register. Check with each store for their policies. With a little organization and some practice, you rarely will pay full price for ANYTHING.

How to organize financial records - many would love to toss receipts and forget about them. However, a crucial part of being able to save, spend less and be fiscally savvy is getting your financial records organized and clear. It means tracking your expenses and writing down your budget. At any given time, you must ascertain where you are within your budget, what you have in your accounts, anything you owe, and your credit score. It helps you to be honest with yourself about where you are financially.

Money management and investing - once your debts are paid off, understanding how to invest your money wisely is a huge learning experience. Even the people with money to spare have trouble with investments and making that money grow. There are very few ways to "get rich quick" short of winning the lottery, and most investing and money management attempts must be carefully vetted and researched, and completed with the assistance of a professional who understands your willingness and risk aversion so they can guide you to the best investments.

Effective negotiation - bargaining, bartering, and negotiating is a learned life skill. Learning to trade, make an offer, and be comfortable with asking for a better deal will save you money. Do not be reluctant about making a bargain. Challenge yourself with practice till you feel comfortable. If that means saying, "Is that the best you can offer?" practice in negotiating will help you learn to stop cringing whenever a negotiating opportunity presents itself.

Self-Awareness Skills

Understanding your calling, purpose, and mission - your higher purpose, your "calling," and what drives you and helps to set the foundation for everything you do. Crafting is not only a family mission statement but a personal mission statement and can help you keep your focus on your most important life goals.

How to prioritize and your priorities - we must learn to prioritize the most important things each day to take care of the most necessary (and often the toughest) tasks. Being able to assess a situation, size it up and figure out what needs to be tackled first.

Understanding your values - like understanding your mission, understanding your values, and refusing to compromise them will guide you through any decision. If honesty is one of your values, you will never be tempted to lie when put in a compromising position because you know honesty is important to you. If family communication and connectedness are a value, you will use that to guide your decisions affecting your children.

How to focus - is twofold: first, how to focus on a task when facing a deadline or when you need to get something done. And second, how to focus your direction, actions, and goals so you are always in line with your values and personal mission.

How to have a sense of humor - parents of tweens are aware of the time in their children's development when the kids start to "get it." Suddenly they can detect subtle tones in conversation, and they learn to be sarcastic and, yes, funny. Some adults struggle with this, but finding the humor in any situation (and even the joy in the toughest ones) will get you far. Humor can help us deal with pain, stress, and problems in life and can help us find the silver lining.

Basic etiquette - understanding basic etiquette remains relevant and vital. Politeness is about consideration for the feelings of others and making sure you do not do something that offends or, frankly, grosses people out.

Relationship Skills

Listening and communication in a partnership - communication in a marriage or relationship (and even with your children) is very different from general communication skills. It is about listening, being unselfish and empathetic, and tackling difficult conversations without prejudice. Words matter, as they can be hurtful or beautiful. They can bring us closer to each other and closer to God, or they can rip us apart. Learning to think before you speak and listen more than you talk are communication tools that will serve you throughout your life and all your close relationships.

Valuing and expressing respect - at the heart of every successful marriage, there is mutual respect. Respecting your spouse and differences can help your marriage become more robust and happier. Learn to view your spouse through the lens of another human being with feelings, desires, and wants that may not always match your own. Understanding the underlying motivations and emotions underneath it all and respecting them as valid will strengthen your marriage.

Valuing and expressing love - is about buying gifts and spoiling your children and spouse, right? WRONG. Love is about quality time, affection, expression, and understanding. To love and to be loved is a life skill that takes work.

How to accept compliments and criticism - receiving compliments and constructive criticism is not easy! Frequently we fail to take compliments with grace or downplay them and get embarrassed, yet we are sometimes crushed by criticisms (even if they are valid) and take them personally and to heart. Learning to say "thank you" when you get a compliment and view criticism as feedback (assess it, then apply it or throw it away) can serve you well.

Emotional intelligence - today's adults have likely heard all the buzz about social-emotional learning. If you are in the business world, you have probably also read a lot about how social and emotional intelligence is important in the workplace. Why is this? Well, people are finding that being emotionally intelligent can be just as important as understanding the nuances of engineering or physics. As the human population grows and we become more global in our interactions, being sensitive to others, understanding emotions, and learning to harness them positively can be a make-or-break life skill. Fortunately, you can work on your emotional intelligence throughout your life and apply it throughout.

How to write thank you messages - thank you notes are a bit of a lost art, but they brighten the day for those who receive them. They are an excellent way to express gratitude and appreciation to others. A thank you note is simple: say thank you for x, y, z, and tell the person how you plan to use their gift or the result of their help. Repeat what it means to you personally, and then close. It is a skill that takes very little time and means so much.

Wellness and Mental Health Skills

Critical thinking and problem-solving - unfortunately, it is not a skill everyone has. This life skill is not about your ability to prioritize but also your ability to break a situation down and make choices. It is about measuring possible outcomes and constructing your thinking skills to tackle life's little bumps.

Synthesizing: a critical thinking skill - is the ability to combine parts of a whole in a new and unique way. This learned skill boosts your adaptability. It is part of the analysis and evaluation of any given situation. This critical thinking skill is "higher-level thinking," something we often slack on after high school or college.

Self-discipline: exercise and nutrition - the ability to discipline yourself enough to make healthy choices about your food and exercise is a learned skill. It is part of "bigger picture" thinking, that is, the understanding that if you eat something now, you might pay for it later.

Self-care: sleep and hygiene - we get so wrapped up in caring for others we forget about the importance of taking care of ourselves. It means sleep and rest, which is critical to our health. It also means taking time, showering, dressing in clean clothing, styling your hair, or doing what you must to feel clean, confident, and at your best. You deserve to feel good.

APPENDIX

ACKNOWLEDGMENT

We acknowledge the following ARTICLES, which provided information for the content of this publication. Additionally, the indicated ORGANIZATIONS are authoritative in the fields of the content presented in this publication.

ARTICLES

10 Healthy Lifestyle Tips for Adults | Eufic
https://www.eufic.org/en/healthy-living/article/10-healthy-lifestyle-tips-for-adults

The 12 Stages of Life | Thomas Armstrong, Ph.D.
https://www.institute4learning.com/resources/articles/the-12-stages-of-life/

12 Personal Hygiene Mistakes Almost Everyone Makes (Mom Never Told You About #4!)
https://naturalon.com/12-personal-hygiene-mistakes-almost-everyone-makes/view-all/

Top 20 Dangerous Foods You Absolutely Must Avoid
https://naturalon.com/top-10-dangerous-foods-you-absolutely-must-avoid/view-all/

48 Essential Life Skills Everyone Should Learn | Life Skills to Master
https://www.livingwellspendingless.com/48-life-skills-everyone-learn/

Allergies - Symptoms and causes - Mayo Clinic
https://www.mayoclinic.org/diseases-conditions/allergies/symptoms-causes/syc-20351497

Allergy medications: Know your options - Mayo Clinic
https://www.mayoclinic.org/diseases-conditions/allergies/in-depth/allergy-medications/art-20047403

Heavy Metals in Baby Food: Should You Worry? - GoodRx
https://www.goodrx.com/well-being/diet-nutrition/heavy-metals-in-baby-food

Teens, Genes, and Food Choices: What Contributes to Adolescent Obesity? | NIDDK
https://www.niddk.nih.gov/health-information/professionals/diabetes-discoveries-practice/teens-genes-and-food-choices

High blood pressure - children: MedlinePlus Medical Encyclopedia
https://medlineplus.gov/ency/article/007696.htm

Why Do My Farts Smell So Bad? - GoodRx
https://www.goodrx.com/conditions/gas/why-do-my-farts-smell-so-bad

Why is family important in a child's development? - ABC Quality
https://www.abcquality.org/posts/2021/why-is-family-important-in-a-childs-development/

ORGANIZATIONS

American Academy of Pediatrics (AAP)
345 Park Boulevard
Itasca, IL 60143
(888) 227-1770 Toll-Free US & Canada
(630) 626-6000 Outside US & Canada
Email: mcc@aap.org
https://www.aap.org/

The American Journal of Clinical Nutrition (AJCN)
https://academic.oup.com/ajcn?

American Society for Nutrition (ASN)
9211 Corporate Boulevard, Suite 300
Rockville, MD 20850
(240) 428-3650

MedlinePlus
National Library of Medicine
8600 Rockville Pike
Bethesda, Maryland 20894
https://medlineplus.gov/

Centers for Disease Control and Prevention (CDC)
1600 Clifton Road
Atlanta, GA 30329-4027
800-232-4636 (800-CDC-INFO)
Email: CDC-INFO Contact Form
https://www.cdc.gov/about/index.html

Mayo Clinic
https://www.mayoclinic.org/about-mayo-clinic/contact
Locations in: Arizona, Florida, Minnesota, London, Abu Dhabi
https://www.mayoclinic.org/healthy-lifestyle
https://www.mayoclinic.org/diseases-conditions
https://www.mayoclinic.org/drugs-supplements
https://www.mayoclinic.org/symptoms
https://www.mayoclinic.org/healthy-lifestyle/stress-management/basics/stress-basics/hlv-20049495

National Institutes of Health (NIH)
9000 Rockville Pike
Bethesda, Maryland 20892
https://www.nih.gov/health-information
301-496-4000
TTY 301-402-9612

ABOUT THE AUTHOR

Pierre Mouchette is a real estate investor, entrepreneur, and author of expository publications on **Real Estate Investing and Investment Knowledge, Environmental Knowledge, Life Knowledge, and Life-Health Knowledge.** All work produced involves critical-thinking skills, the ability to simplify complex, technical information for consumers with nontechnical backgrounds, research, analysis, and input from industry experts and national organizations. Publications explain, inform, describe, and present concepts in simple, understandable language. Expository content is appropriately structured in **Books, Manuals, Guides, and How-to-Articles.**

For more information on Pierre, click here.
{https://www.synchronicity-investor.com/about-author.html}.

THE TEAM

We acknowledge the following individuals who read our unpublished manuscript before its final editing. These Team Members are within the target audience and have volunteered to read the manuscript and give honest feedback on its contents. The Team Members take our work from good but not ready for publication to being prepared for a final edit.

CREDITS:	
Alpha	Tomasa M. Mouchette
Beta	

AFTERWORD

Thank You For Reading,

HUMAN DEVELOPMENT

A Guide By The Numbers
For Health and Wellness

We hope you enjoyed this
Enviro | Life Knowledge Publication

Thank you again, valued reader,
And we hope to meet you again on another book.

Suggested Reading:

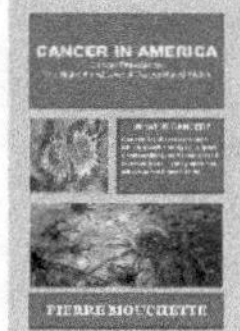

CANCER IN AMERICA

Cancer Prevalence, And The Highest and Lowest Cancer Rated States

We all know food is essential for keeping the body healthy and fit. Healthy food habits keep our bodies free from toxins, free radicals, nutrient deprivation, and certain diseases.

Cancer is a complex disease with many types and potential causes. Although we still do not know all the answers, various factors can contribute to cancer development. Genetic structure and family history play a role. But external factors, such as lifestyle habits, have an even more significant impact.

The most crucial lifestyle factor for consideration is your diet. Research shows that some foods are associated with a higher risk of specific types of cancer. Some foods may increase your risk of type 2 diabetes and obesity, associated with certain types of cancer. Other food products can contain carcinogens, which are harmful substances that can cause cancer.

What Are Nitrates?

The Good, The Bad, and The Alternatives

Depending on where they are sourced from, nitrates can help or hinder your health. Support your overall health by eating whole foods, fresh fruits, and vegetables which can benefit cardiovascular health, blood flow to the brain, and body balance.

A healthy diet can diminish chronic illness and the onset of certain diseases, such as colorectal and gastric cancer.